SPORTS SUPE

TOM BRADY

By Kevin Frederickson

Kaleidoscope
Minneapolis, MN

Your Front Row Seat to the Games

This edition is co-published by agreement between
Kaleidoscope and World Book, Inc.

Kaleidoscope Publishing, Inc.
6012 Blue Circle Drive
Minnetonka, MN 55343 U.S.A.

World Book, Inc.
180 North LaSalle St., Suite 900
Chicago IL 60601 U.S.A.

Kaleidoscope ISBNs
978-1-64519-050-9 (library binding)
978-1-64494-207-9 (paperback)
978-1-64519-151-3 (ebook)

World Book ISBN
978-0-7166-4354-8 (library bound)

Library of Congress Control Number
2019940069

Printed in the United States of America.

TABLE OF
CONTENTS

CHAPTER 1

A Historic Comeback

Things were not going well for Tom Brady. One Atlanta Falcons player intercepted his pass. Another knocked Brady to the ground. All the New England Patriots quarterback could do was watch. The Falcons ran the ball back for a touchdown. That put them up 28–3. And nearly an entire half remained in the Super Bowl on February 5, 2017.

All hope appeared lost. No team had ever come back from this far behind in a Super Bowl. But no team was quite like the Patriots. In the third quarter, Brady got to work. He led the Patriots to Atlanta's 5-yard line. Brady threw a short pass to James White. The running back **deked** a few defenders. Then he ran the ball in for a touchdown. Now New England trailed 28–9.

FUN FACT

Before February 2017, the biggest comeback in Super Bowl history was 10 points.

Atlanta's Robert Alford races away from Tom Brady after making an interception in Super Bowl LI.

The Patriots didn't stop there. They kicked a field goal. Then Brady threw for another touchdown. Just like that, the Patriots now trailed 28–20. New England began its next drive at its 9-yard line. Brady marched the team down the field. They scored another touchdown. But only 57 seconds remained. The Patriots needed a two-point conversion.

Calm under pressure, Brady completes the two-point conversion pass to Danny Amendola.

Brady threw a short pass to his left. Danny Amendola caught it. He was just short of the end zone. So he charged forward across the goal line. Tie game!

It was on to overtime.

Once Brady got rolling in Super Bowl LI, he couldn't be stopped.

By now Brady and the Patriots were rolling. They drove to the 2-yard line. Brady took the snap. He pitched the ball to White. The speedy running back raced to the outside. Then he cut back in. Finally, he dove across the goal line. Touchdown! Brady could hardly believe it. Soon he was surrounded by his teammates. New England had won 34–28.

Brady had good reason to celebrate. He had just led the greatest comeback in Super Bowl history. He also won his fifth Super Bowl. No one had won more.

FUN FACT
Brady was named Super Bowl Most Valuable Player (MVP) for the fourth time.

CHAPTER 2

Tom grew up near San Francisco, California.

California Dreaming

A young Tom Brady finds his seat. It's January 10, 1982. He's at a San Francisco 49ers game. They are his favorite team. And this is a huge game. A win would send San Francisco to the Super Bowl. But time is running out. The 49ers need a touchdown.

FUN FACT

The famous play Tom watched on that 1982 day is now simply known as "The Catch."

49ers quarterback Joe Montana drops back to pass. His throw is high. It looks like it will sail out of the end zone. Instead, Dwight Clark stretches out and grabs it. Touchdown! The 49ers win. They are going to the Super Bowl. Tom called it a "magical time." He wanted to be just like Montana.

Where Brady Has Been

1 **San Mateo, California:** Brady was born here on August 3, 1977.

2 **Ann Arbor, Michigan:** Brady played college football here for the University of Michigan from 1996–99.

3 **Foxborough, Massachusetts:** Where Brady and the Patriots play.

4 **New Orleans, Louisiana:** Brady and the Patriots beat the St. Louis Rams to win New England's first Super Bowl here on February 3, 2002.

5 **Houston, Texas:** Where Brady led the comeback from 28–3 against the Falcons on February 5, 2017.

6 **Atlanta, Georgia:** On February 3, 2019, Brady won his sixth Super Bowl here.

Tom was born on August 3, 1977, in San Mateo, California. Growing up, he played a lot of sports. In high school, Tom played baseball and football. He wasn't always a star for Junipero Serra High School. He began on the ninth-grade team. And he was a backup. But he worked hard. Later he became the **varsity** starting quarterback. He threw for more than 3,000 yards in high school. The team named him MVP during his senior year.

Tom was also a really good catcher in baseball. Some thought he could play professionally. The Montreal Expos wanted him. They selected Tom in the 1995 Major League Baseball (MLB) **Draft**.

San Mateo is on San Francisco Bay, just south of San Francisco.

Tom prepares to take a snap during a 1999 Michigan Wolverines game.

Tom enjoyed baseball. Football was his true passion, though. The University of Michigan offered him a **scholarship**. Tom accepted it. Michigan has one of the country's top football programs. But Tom struggled early on. Again, he began as a backup. But he kept working. After two years, he was ready to start.

The 1998 Wolverines had a rocky start. They began with two losses. Then Tom led the team to ten wins in their final eleven games.

In 1999, Tom had competition for his job. Another quarterback sometimes played, too. But Tom started every game. He led the team to a 10–2 record. In the Orange Bowl, Michigan trailed Alabama 14–0. Tom ended on a high note. He led a comeback. The Wolverines forced overtime. Then they won 35–34.

FUN FACT
The 1997 Wolverines won the national title during Tom's sophomore year.

15

CHAPTER 3

More Than Just a Player

A saxophone player plays. Brady walks onto the stage. The crowd cheers. It's April 16, 2005. Brady is hosting *Saturday Night Live*. The popular TV show begins with a **monologue**. There is no football in sight. Yet Brady looks right at home. He tells jokes. He even sings. Afterward, Brady acts in **skits**.

Football helped Brady become popular. That led to opportunities off the field. Brady has embraced them. He has appeared on other TV shows. He's also written a book.

FUN FACT

In 2018, Brady filmed a web series about his life called *Tom vs. Time.*

Saturday Night Live *is filmed at New York City's famous Rockefeller Center.*

CAREER TIMELINE

1977

August 3, 1977
Tom Brady is born in San Mateo, California.

January 10, 1982
Brady watches "The Catch" at Candlestick Park in San Francisco, California.

1982

June 1995
The Montreal Expos select Brady in the 18th round of the MLB Draft.

1995

September 28, 1996
Brady appears in his first game with the University of Michigan football team.

1996

2000

April 16, 2000
The Patriots take Brady in the sixth round of the NFL Draft.

February 3, 2002
Brady leads New England to its first Super Bowl win, beating the favored St. Louis Rams.

2002

February 5, 2017
Brady leads the Patriots to a win in the Super Bowl after trailing 28–3 in the third quarter.

2017

February 3, 2019
Brady wins his record sixth Super Bowl with New England.

2019

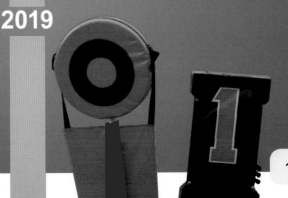

Brady uses football as a way to help others. He has worked with **charities**. One is called Best Buddies. It helps people with mental or physical disabilities. In June 2018, Best Buddies held a football game. Brady played with kids in the program. Some of his Patriots teammates joined him.

Brady congratulates a teammate during a Best Buddies Challenge charity football game.

A FAMOUS DUO

Gisele Bündchen was world famous before she married Brady. She grew up in Brazil. At 19, she began modeling for Victoria's Secret. It sells undergarments and pajamas. Bündchen became the world's top-earning model. She held that position for fifteen straight years. In 2009, she married Brady. They have two kids together. Brady also has a son with a former girlfriend.

The TB12 Method helps Brady stay in great shape.

Football is at the center of Brady's life. He is always preparing. One way he gets ready is eating healthy. He even has his own **diet**. It's called the TB12 Method. Brady drinks a lot of water. He eats lots of fruits, vegetables, and proteins. Brady believes this will help him stay in shape. That way, he can play football for a long time.

FUN FACT

As part of the TB12 Method, Brady eats ice cream made out of avocados.

CHAPTER 4

All-Time Great

Brady completes a pass to J. R. Redmond for 11 yards. The Patriots are 41 yards from the end zone. But less than a minute remains in the Super Bowl. The Patriots and St. Louis Rams are tied 17–17. So Brady and his team keep going. Brady completes two more passes. Now they are 30 yards from the end zone. But only seven seconds remain. Brady's work on February 3, 2002, is done.

Adam Vinatieri takes the field. The Patriots' kicker sends the ball right through the **uprights.** New England has won its first Super Bowl. Few could believe it. The fact that Brady led the way was even more surprising.

FUN FACT

NFL teams picked 198 players in the 2000 draft before the Patriots selected Brady.

Few could believe it when Brady led the Patriots into Super Bowl XXXVI against the St. Louis Rams.

Brady was a backup. Most thought he would remain one. Then the Patriots' starter got hurt early in the season. Brady took over. Suddenly, the Patriots couldn't lose. But the Rams were really good. They were big favorites to win the Super Bowl. Instead, Brady proved he was the real deal. And his career was only beginning.

The Patriots won two more Super Bowls in the next three seasons. Those teams relied on strong defenses. The 2007 team had a great defense, too. But it also had a killer offense. Brady had lots of talented teammates. And he used them. The Patriots averaged 37 points per game. Brady threw 50 touchdowns. And his team won its first 18 games. But the Patriots lost the biggest one, the Super Bowl.

Life was good for Brady after leading the Patriots to another Super Bowl title in February 2004.

CAREER
STATS

TOUCHDOWN PASSES	**517**
PASSING YARDS	**70,514**
INTERCEPTIONS	**171**
COMPLETION PERCENTAGE	**64%**
PASSER RATING	**97.6**
GAMES PLAYED	**267**

Brady's teammates kept changing. But Brady kept winning. In 2018, he was 41 years old. People wondered when he would slow down. Brady kept them waiting.

The Patriots won 11 games. Then they reached another Super Bowl. It was Brady's ninth appearance. The Patriots faced the Rams again. That team now played in Los Angeles. Quarterback Jared Goff led the Rams. He was just 24 years old. But Brady showed why he was still the best. The Patriots won 13–3. He began his career as a backup. Now he had six Super Bowl wins. No player had more.

DEFLATEGATE

In 2015, Brady got in trouble. The Indianapolis Colts noticed something. His footballs were not fully filled with air. That made it easier for him to pass. But it was against the rules. The league suspended Brady for four games.

No player and team in NFL history have had the success that Brady and the Patriots have.

FUN FACT
Brady won two of his six Super Bowls in Houston, Texas.

BEYOND
THE BOOK

After reading the book, it's time to think about what you learned.
Try the following exercises to jumpstart your ideas.

THINK

THAT'S NEWS TO ME. Brady won six Super Bowls between the 2001 and 2018 seasons. How might news sources be able to fill in more detail about this run of success? What new information could you find in news articles? Where could you go to find those sources?

CREATE

PRIMARY SOURCES. A primary source is a first-hand account. Make a list of different primary sources you might be able to find about Brady. What new information might you learn from these sources?

SHARE

SUM IT UP. Write one paragraph summarizing the important points from this book. Make sure it's in your own words. Don't just copy what is in the text. Share the paragraph with a classmate. Does your classmate have any comments about the summary? What other questions does he or she have about Brady?

GROW

REAL-LIFE RESEARCH. What places could you visit to learn more about Brady? What other things could you learn while you were there?

RESEARCH NINJA

Visit *www.ninjaresearcher.com/0509* to learn how
to take your research skills and book report writing to the next level!

RESEARCH

DIGITAL LITERACY TOOLS

SEARCH LIKE A PRO
Learn about how to use search engines to find useful websites.

FACT OR FAKE?
Discover how you can tell a trusted website from an untrustworthy resource.

TEXT DETECTIVE
Explore how to zero in on the information you need most.

SHOW YOUR WORK
Research responsibly— learn how to cite sources.

WRITE

GET TO THE POINT
Learn how to express your main ideas.

PLAN OF ATTACK
Learn prewriting exercises and create an outline.

DOWNLOADABLE REPORT FORMS

Further Resources

BOOKS

Fishman, Jon M. *Football Superstar Tom Brady*. Lerner, 2019.

Whiting, Jim. *The Story of the New England Patriots*. Creative Education, 2019.

Wilner, Barry. *Tom Brady and the New England Patriots*. Abdo Publishing, 2019.

WEBSITES

FACTSURFER

Factsurfer.com gives you a safe, fun way to find more information.

1. Go to www.factsurfer.com.

2. Enter "Tom Brady" into the search box and click 🔍.

3. Select your book cover to see a list of related websites.

Glossary

charities: Charities are organizations that help people in need. Brady works with many charities.

deked: To deke someone means to fake going one way then go the other. Brady deked a defender and kept running down the field.

diet: A diet is what someone eats or drinks. Brady's diet includes lots of water and avocado ice cream.

draft: A draft is an event when teams in a sports league take turns selecting players who are new to the league. The Montreal Expos baseball team selected Brady in the MLB Draft.

monologue: A monologue is a long speech given by one person. *Saturday Night Live* opens with a funny monologue by the host.

scholarship: A scholarship is an award that helps a student pay for college. The University of Michigan awarded Brady a scholarship to play football there.

skits: Skits are when a group of people perform a show making fun of something. Brady appeared in skits when he was on *Saturday Night Live*.

uprights: In football, the uprights are what make up the goal post where kickers try to kick the ball through. The Patriots' kicker sent the ball through the uprights for a field goal.

varsity: A varsity team is the best team in a given sport at a high school. By his senior year, Brady starred on the varsity football team.

Index

PHOTO CREDITS

The images in this book are reproduced through the courtesy of: Paul Jasienski/AP Images, front cover (center); Jeff Roberson/AP Images, front cover (right), p. 3; EFKS/Shutterstock Images, front cover (background top), front cover (background bottom); Ric Tapia/AP Images, p. 5; Aaron M. Sprecher/AP Images, pp. 6–7; Gregory Payan/AP Images, p. 8; Elise Amendola/AP Images, p. 9; canadastock/Shutterstock Images, pp. 10–11; Phil Huber/Dallas Morning News/AP Images, p. 11; Red Line Editorial, pp. 12, 25 (chart); Sundry Photography/Shutterstock Images, p. 13; Scott Boehm/AP Images, pp. 14–15; Sean Pavone/Shutterstock Images, p. 16; Mtsaride/Shutterstock Images, pp. 17 (top), 30; saje/iStockphoto, p. 17 (bottom); Michael Dwyer/AP Images, p. 18; Sky Cinema/Shutterstock Images, p. 19; Mark Lennihan/AP Images, p. 20; Brent Hofacker/Shutterstock, p. 21 (left); Lipskiy/Shutterstock Images, p. 21 (right); Tom DiPace/AP Images, pp. 22–23; Dave Martin/AP Images, p. 24; Jim Mahoney/AP Images, p. 25 (Tom Brady); Charlie Neibergall/AP Images, pp. 26–27.

ABOUT THE AUTHOR

Kevin Frederickson is a freelance writer and editor from Ohio. He lives near Cincinnati with his golden doodle, Max.